"Surviving Hyperinflation"

A practical guide from personal experience

By
Ahmed F. Yassin
An Eyewitness of Iraq 1990s Hyperinflation

Table Of Contents

Dedication

To my beloved family members back home in Iraq, who have supported me every step of the way, this book is dedicated to you. Your unwavering love and encouragement have been a constant source of inspiration for me.

To my two wonderful American families, the Stanley and Costa families, who welcomed me with open arms, loved and cared for me always, I am forever grateful. This book is a testament to the kindness and generosity you have shown me, and I dedicate it to you with all my heart.

To all mankind and all of those interested to learn about Hyperinflation and economy and take effective measures to protect themselves and their loved ones, this book is for you. May it serve as a guide and a warning, urging us to be vigilant and proactive in safeguarding our economic well-being.

To all of my friends who have encouraged me, helped shape my thoughts, and provided feedback on this humble work, I extend my heartfelt thanks. Without your unwavering support and encouragement, this book would not have been possible.

Sincerely, Ahmed F. Yassin.

Introduction

The 1990s were a difficult and tumultuous time for the people of Iraq. One of the major challenges that the country faced during this period was a severe economic crisis known as hyperinflation.

Hyperinflation is a rapid and out-of-control increase in prices, and it can have devastating consequences for a country's economy and its people. In the case of Iraq, the hyperinflation of the 1990s was the result of a number of factors, including political instability, economic sanctions, and mismanagement of the country's resources.

The root cause of Iraq's hyperinflation can be traced back to the 1980s, when the country was engaged in a long and costly war with its neighbor, Iran. The war drained Iraq's resources and led to a rise in government spending. Also, the other main cause of hyperinflation in Iraq during this time was the country's ongoing economic sanctions, which had been imposed by the United Nations following the Gulf War. These sanctions restricted Iraq's ability to trade with other countries, leading to a lack of foreign currency and a shortage of goods. Additionally, Iraq's infrastructure was severely damaged during the war, which further exacerbated the country's economic woes.

The reconstruction efforts in Iraq following the Gulf War, combined with international economic sanctions on oil exports, greatly impacted the country's economy and led to a period of hyperinflation in the 1990s. The loss of such a significant portion of country's revenue resulted in the Iraqi central bank issuing more dinars to meet their annual budget, ultimately speeding up the rate of hyperinflation.

The social and economic consequences of hyperinflation in Iraq during the 1990s were severe and devastating. The country's currency, the Iraqi dinar, lost value rapidly, with the exchange rate reaching an all-time low of around 3,000 dinars to one US dollar at the peak of the inflation. Furthermore, the prices for goods and services were skyrocketing. According to some estimates, the inflation rate reached as high as 7,000% at its peak. Housing prices and wages also plummeted, making it difficult for people to afford basic necessities like food and medicine. Many Iraqis were forced to live in poverty, and the country's social fabric was severely damaged as people struggled to make ends meet. Many families lost their savings as the value of the dinar plummeted, and many were forced to live in extreme poverty.

Overall, the social and economic consequences of hyperinflation were far-reaching and long-lasting, and most consequences continued to be felt until today. But, despite these challenges, the Iraqi people have remained resilient and have worked tirelessly to rebuild their country and their lives.

What is inflation and hyperinflations means, how it relates to currency?

Inflation is an economic term that refers to the general rise in prices of goods and services over time. When prices increase = the value of money decreases, meaning that it will take more money to buy the same goods and services as before. Inflation is measured by the Consumer Price Index (CPI)[1], which tracks changes in the prices of a basket of goods and services over time.

Hyperinflation is a special type of inflation where the rate of increase in prices is exceptionally high and starts to spiral out of control. Hyperinflation is typically defined as an inflation rate of over 50% per month [2]. When hyperinflation occurs, the value of money falls quickly, and it becomes difficult for people to afford basic necessities, like food and housing.

Hyperinflation is often caused by over-issuance of currency. When a government or central bank prints too much money, it can lead to an oversupply of currency, which can cause prices to increase rapidly. This oversupply of money can be caused by a variety of factors, including government overspending, war, and economic mismanagement.

During hyperinflation, it is not that the prices of goods and services rise, but the value of the currency reduces, which makes prices look like they are rising, but in reality, the currency is losing its value. For example, if you had 100 dollars before hyperinflation, it can buy you a certain amount of goods, but during hyperinflation, the same 100 dollars can buy you significantly less goods, because the value of the currency has reduced.

One of the most famous historical examples of hyperinflation occurred in Germany in the 1920s. After World War I, Germany was heavily in debt, and the government began printing money to pay off its debts. This led to an oversupply of currency, which caused prices to skyrocket. In 1923, prices were increasing at a rate of more than 20% per day, and by the end of the year, it was estimated that prices had increased by around 4.2 trillion%. This made the German currency, the Reichsmark, effectively worthless, and people were forced to use wheelbarrows full of money to buy basic necessities [4].

Another example of hyperinflation occurred in Zimbabwe in the 2000s. Zimbabwe's economy was in a state of collapse, and the government began printing money to pay for its expenses. This led to an oversupply of currency, which caused prices to skyrocket. In 2008, prices were increasing at a rate of more than 100,000% per year, and by the end of the year, it was estimated that prices had increased by around 79.6 billion %. This made the Zimbabwean currency, the Zimbabwean dollar, effectively worthless, and people were forced to use foreign currencies like the US dollar to buy goods and services.

In conclusion, hyperinflation is an economic term that refers to the general rise in prices of goods and services over time, where the rate of increase in prices is exceptionally high and starts to spiral out of control. It is often caused by an over-issuance of currency, which leads to an oversupply of money and causes prices to increase rapidly. During hyperinflation, the value of money falls quickly, and it becomes difficult for people to afford basic necessities causing social and economic consequences [3].

References:

1. Bureau of Labor Statistics (BLS). (n.d.). Consumer Price Index (CPI). Retrieved from https://www.bls.gov/cpi/

2. Hanke, S. H. (2019). Hyperinflation: A world-historical perspective. Cato Journal, 39(2), 287-296.

3. International Monetary Fund. (2009). Hyperinflation in Zimbabwe. Retrieved from https://www.imf.org/external/pubs/cat/longres.aspx?sk=23028.0

4. Federal Reserve Bank of St. Louis. (n.d.). The German Hyperinflation, 1923-1924. Retrieved from https://www.stlouisfed.org/~/media/files/pdfs/great-depression/german-hyperinflation.pdf

What can we do about it? And How?

Hyperinflation is a serious economic problem that can have a devastating impact on people's lives. As prices for goods and services soar, it can become increasingly difficult for people to afford basic necessities, like food and housing. The value of savings and pensions can also be rapidly eroded, making it difficult for people to plan for the future.

It is important to understand that hyperinflation is often caused by larger economic and political factors that are outside of an individual's control. However, there are steps that people can take to mitigate the effects of hyperinflation and protect their financial well-being.

To survive hyperinflation, it's important to manage expenses and create a budget, save in stable currency or forms not affected by inflation, increase income, diversify income, reduce debt, build an emergency fund, and prioritize necessities over luxuries. These steps will be discussed in more detail in upcoming chapters.

In Iraq during this time, the public was tragically uninformed about the looming threat of hyperinflation. They believed in the strength of the Iraqi dinar, and there were no reliable sources of information to educate them about the dire consequences of hyperinflation. Unfortunately, with the country already having suffered through a devastating war and subsequent unrest, any chance of preparation was essentially impossible. The markets and basic infrastructure had been decimated, leaving little room for proactive measures.

Thus, the only options available to the people were to rely on owning real estate or precious metal jewelry. As it was a cultural norm that the gold was often gifted or purchased for weddings. Unlike in the United States, where the government mints can sell precious metal coins and bars directly to the public, resources were extremely limited in this situation, and were quickly depleted within the first year of hyperinflation.

In summary, hyperinflation is a dire economic situation that can have a severe impact on individuals' lives. It is often caused by larger economic and political forces that are beyond an individual's control. However, there are steps that can be taken to reduce the impact of hyperinflation and safeguard one's financial well-being.

To avoid experiencing the devastating effects of hyperinflation in any society, it is crucial to be well-informed and prepared in advance. This guide is designed to help increase awareness and provide preparation strategies, so that the mistakes of the past are not repeated.

"Here are the top 10 steps to increase your chances of surviving hyperinflation."

1. Budgeting and cost management:

Budgeting and cost management are critical for surviving hyperinflation as they assist households in reducing their reliance on cash and making people aware of the prices of essential items in the market. While these tips and ideas for effectively managing expenses and creating a budget during hyperinflation are universal, it's important to keep in mind that in the case of Iraq, the country's prior period of wars and political instability hindered the ability to implement some of these strategies.

1. **Track your expenses:** Keeping track of all your expenses, including how much you're spending on necessities like food and rent, as well as discretionary expenses like entertainment and clothing, will give you a clear picture of where your money is going.

2. **Set financial goals:** Setting financial goals, such as saving a certain amount of money each month or paying off a specific debt, can help you prioritize your expenses and

make sure that you're using your money in a way that aligns with your values and priorities.

3. **Make a budget:** Once you have a clear picture of your expenses, create a budget that allocates your money in a way that aligns with your financial goals. Be sure to include a contingency for unexpected expenses.

4. **Prioritize expenses:** Prioritize expenses by determining which are essential and which are not. Cut back on non-essential expenses as much as possible to free up money for essentials.

5. **Look for ways to save:** Look for ways to save money on essential expenses, such as by shopping around for the best prices on groceries or by negotiating with landlords for a lower rent.

6. **Create a buffer:** Create a buffer of extra money in your budget to account for unexpected expenses or fluctuations in prices.

7. **Monitor your budget regularly:** Monitor your budget regularly and make adjustments as needed. Keep in mind that prices may fluctuate frequently during times of hyperinflation, so you may need to adjust your budget more often than usual.

8. **Be realistic:** Be realistic about what you can afford. Don't stretch yourself too thin, as this can lead to more debt and financial difficulties.

9. **Seek help:** If you find it difficult to manage your expenses or create a budget, seek help from a financial advisor or a budget counselor.

10. **Be flexible:** Be flexible and open to making changes to your budget as the situation evolves. Remember that hyperinflation can bring sudden changes in prices, and sometimes you may have to change your budget to adapt to new circumstances.

In summary, budgeting and cost management are crucial during times of hyperinflation because they help households reduce their dependence on cash by allowing them to carefully manage their expenses and make sure that their money is being used in a way that aligns with their values and priorities. By tracking expenses, setting financial goals, creating a budget, looking for ways to save, monitoring the budget regularly and being flexible, households can increase their chances of surviving hyperinflation.

2. Building savings

Building savings in a stable currency or in a form that is not easily affected by inflation, such as gold or real estate, can help preserve wealth during hyperinflation.

Building savings is an important strategy for surviving hyperinflation because it can help preserve wealth by protecting it from the eroding effects of inflation.

In Iraq, as previously stated, wars and years of hardship have prevented Iraqis from developing a sustainable savings system to protect them during times of hyperinflation. As a result, they had to rely on the small savings they had in Iraqi dinar, which were severely devalued when the currency fell. For example, my father used to have 10,000 Iraqi dinars saved for emergencies, which was equivalent to 25,000 or 30,000 dollars. However, due to lack of knowledge about the reality of hyperinflation and the absence of a guide like this, the value of my father's savings dropped to only $50-$100. If my father had known about this, he could have used his savings to purchase gold jewelry, preserving or even increasing the value of his currency over time. Therefore, it is crucial to read a comprehensive guide like this one and apply what is available to you before the situation worsens.

Below are some general examples, tips, and ideas for how to effectively build savings during times of hyperinflation:

1. **Open a savings account in a stable currency**: One way to preserve wealth during hyperinflation is to save money in a currency that is not affected by inflation. For example, opening a savings account in a currency like the US dollar or Euro can help protect your money from inflation.

2. **Invest in gold or other precious metals**: Another option for preserving wealth during hyperinflation is to invest in gold or other precious metals, which have historically been a store of value and a hedge against inflation.

3. **Invest in real estate**: Investing in real estate can also be a good way to preserve wealth during hyperinflation because property prices tend to increase with inflation.

4. **Save regularly**: Set up automatic savings plan to save a certain amount of money each month, even if it is a small amount.

5. **Start early**: The earlier you start saving, the more time you will have to build wealth, which in turn give you better chance to build savings.

6. **Make saving a priority**: Make saving a priority by allocating a certain percentage of your income to savings each month.

7. **Diversify your savings**: Diversify your savings by spreading your money across different savings accounts, investments, and assets.

8. **Avoid high-risk investments**: Avoid high-risk investments that may be more likely to lose value during times of hyperinflation.

9. **Seek professional advice**: If you are unsure of where to invest your money, seek advice from a financial advisor or investment professional.

10. **Be patient**: Building savings takes time and patience. Be prepared to wait for your investments to grow and don't expect to get rich quick.

In summary, building savings is an important strategy for surviving hyperinflation because it can help preserve wealth by protecting it from the eroding effects of inflation. By opening a savings account in a stable currency, investing in gold or other precious metals, investing in real estate, saving regularly, starting early, making saving a priority, diversifying savings, avoiding high-risk investments, seeking professional advice and being patient, individuals can increase their chances of preserving wealth during hyperinflation.

3. Increasing income

**Finding additional sources of income can provide
more cash to survive hyperinflation.**

Increasing one's income is a crucial strategy for surviving hyperinflation, as it allows for more funds to be allocated towards paying for essential expenses. In the western world, it is common for individuals to take on multiple jobs in order to financially sustain themselves. During the 90s in Iraq, we had to get creative and utilize our skills, time, and networks to seek out opportunities that would bring in additional funds to cover the expenses of daily living, such as rent and food. These included utilizing the universal tips below, such as taking on a second job, rent out a space room, sell items or furniture, take a freelance work, take advantage of any government assistance, and finally, networking with others seeking out new opportunities to increase income.

Here are some universal examples, tips, and ideas for how to effectively increase income during times of hyperinflation:

1. **Get a second job**: Finding a second job, even if it is part-time or temporary, can provide additional income to help pay for expenses.

2. **Start a side business**: Starting a small business or becoming self-employed can also provide additional income. This could be something as simple as selling items online or providing a service to your community.

3. **Rent out a spare room**: If you have a spare room in your home, consider renting it out to a tenant. This can provide additional income without requiring a significant time commitment.

4. **Sell items you no longer need**: Take an inventory of items that you no longer need or use and sell them to earn extra money.

5. **Invest in stocks or bonds**: Investing in stocks or bonds can provide additional income through dividends or interest payments.

6. **Look for ways to monetize your skills or talents**: Teach a class or offer consulting services.

7. **Take on freelance work**: Look for freelance work that can be done from home or on a flexible schedule.

8. **Negotiate a raise**: If you are currently employed, consider negotiating a raise with your employer.

9. **Take advantage of government assistance programs**: Look for government assistance programs that can provide

additional income, such as unemployment benefits, food stamps, and other social assistance programs.

10. **Network**: Networking with other professionals in your field can open up new job or business opportunities.

In summary, increasing income is an important strategy for surviving hyperinflation because it can provide more cash to help pay for basic necessities and preserve wealth. By getting a second job, starting a side business, renting out a spare room, selling items you no longer need, investing in stocks or bonds, looking for ways to monetize your skills or talents, taking on freelance work, negotiating a raise, taking advantage of government assistance programs and networking, people can increase their chances of surviving hyperinflation.

4. Diversifying income

Having multiple sources of income can reduce the impact of any one income source failing.

Diversifying one's income sources is a key strategy for surviving hyperinflation, as it helps to mitigate the risk of any single income source failing. By having multiple sources of income, individuals can ensure that they have a consistent flow of cash, even if one source dries up. This approach is particularly useful in developed countries, where there are more opportunities to diversify income through stock markets and other programs. In Iraq, we similarly employed the strategy of increasing income, but also sought out additional sources of income to diversify and protect ourselves from the impact of hyperinflation.

Below are the most common examples, tips, and ideas for how to effectively diversify income during times of hyperinflation:

1. **Have a mix of different types of income**: Having a mix of different types of income, such as wages, investments, and

rental income, can provide a buffer against any other failing income source.

2. **Diversify investments**: Diversifying investments, such as spreading money across different stocks, bonds, and real estate, can help to reduce the impact the one investment that is failing.

3. **Consider multiple streams of passive income**: Rent properties, invest in dividend-paying stocks, or interest-bearing accounts.

4. **Start a side hustle**: Starting a side hustle, such as a small business or freelance work, can provide additional income without requiring a significant time commitment.

5. **Look for ways to monetize hobbies or interests**: Sell crafts, provide photography services, or monetize any other skills you might have.

6. **Rent out assets**: Rent out cars or equipment to generate additional income.

7. **Look for government benefits or assistance program**: Look for unemployment benefits, disability benefits, Veterans assistance program and others.

8. **Look for part-time or seasonal work**: During times of need, look into seasonal or part-time work.

9. **Save and invest**: Saving and investing a portion of your income can provide a source of passive income in the future.

10. **Network**: Networking with other professionals in your field or industry can open up new job or business opportunities.

It is important to note that diversifying income does not guarantee safety from hyperinflation;however it can help to spread the risk of losing all income in case one source fails.

In summary, diversifying income is an important strategy for surviving hyperinflation because it can reduce the impact of the income source that fails. By having a mix of different types of income, diversifying investments, having multiple streams of passive income, starting a side hustle, looking for ways to monetize hobbies or interests, renting out assets, looking for government benefits, looking for part-time or seasonal work, saving, investing, and networking, people can increase their chances of surviving hyperinflation by spreading the risk of losing all income in case one fails.

5. Reducing debt

Paying off or reducing debt as much as possible can help reduce the amount of money that needs to be paid in interest.

To survive hyperinflation, reducing debt is crucial as it lowers interest payments. With high inflation, the value of money decreases, making it harder to pay off debts. By reducing or paying off debt, people can have more cash for necessities and chance to survive economic hardship. In Iraq, the lack of a banking system and credit cards system means that individuals are less affected by debt. However, some business loans had inflated prices of services and products as a result of businessmen attempt to payback those loans. Here are some universal tips to effectively reduce debt during hyperinflation.

1. **Make a budget**: Make a budget and track expenses to identify areas where money is being wasted. Cut back on unnecessary expenses and use the extra money to pay off debt.

2. **Prioritize debt payments**: Prioritize debt payments by starting with the debt with the highest interest rate first. This will help to reduce the amount of money that needs to be paid in interest over time.

3. **Negotiate with creditors**: Negotiate with creditors to lower interest rates or extend the terms of debt.

4. **Consolidate debt**: Consolidate debt by taking out a loan to pay off multiple debts at once. This can help to simplify debt payments and reduce the amount of money that needs to be paid in interest.

5. **Seek professional help**: Seek professional help from a financial advisor or credit counselor to create a debt repayment plan.

6. **Avoid new debt**: Avoid taking on new debt, such as credit card balances or loans, during times of hyperinflation.

7. **Make extra payments**: Make extra payments towards debt when possible.

8. **Look for government assistance programs**: Look for government assistance programs that can help with debt repayment, such as debt forgiveness or debt consolidation programs.

In summary, reducing debt is an important strategy for surviving hyperinflation because it can help to reduce the amount of money that needs to be paid in interest. By making a budget, prioritizing debt payments, negotiating with creditors, consolidating debt, seeking professional help, avoiding new debt, making extra payments and looking for government assistance programs, people can increase their chances of   surviving

hyperinflation by freeing up more cash to pay for basic necessities and preserve wealth.

6. Building an emergency fund

Building an emergency fund can provide a source of cash during crisis.

Building an emergency fund is crucial for surviving life's ups and downs, as it's a common practice recommended by cultures worldwide. This is also true in Iraq, where people save what they can, based on their financial abilities. However, the rapid decline of the Iraqi dinar caught many off guard, leading to loss of savings and emergency funds for those who couldn't convert to stable assets in time. In times of hyperinflation, prices can soar unexpectedly, making it hard to budget for unexpected expenses. Having an emergency fund (and a diverse one, even better) offers a financial cushion to cover those expenses and avoid taking on debt. Though, it is definitely challenging to save while living paycheck to paycheck, it will be worth it as the recent hyperinflation experience in Iraq serves as a stark reminder of the importance of having an emergency fund.

Here are most common examples for how to build an emergency fund during times of hyperinflation:

1. **Start small**: Start small by setting a realistic goal for how much money you want to save and then work towards that goal over time.

2. **Automate savings**: Automate savings by setting up automatic monthly/ biweekly transfers from your checking account to a savings account.

3. **Look for ways to save money**: Look for ways to save money, such as by cutting back on unnecessary expenses or finding ways to increase income.

4. **Avoid dipping into emergency funds**: Try not to access the emergency fund for non-emergency expenses.

5. **Keep emergency funds in a safe and accessible place**: To ensure the availability of funds during an emergency, it is advisable to keep them in a secure and easily accessible location, such as a savings account.

6. **Keep building the fund**: Keep building the fund even after reaching the goal. The value of money decrease during hyperinflation, so you will need more money to cover expenses in the future.

7. **Consider keeping some money in a stable currency**: Consider keeping some money in a stable currency or in a form that is not easily affected by inflation, such as gold or real estate, in case of emergency.

8. **Have a plan**: Have a plan for how the emergency funds will be used in case of an emergency.

To sum up, having an emergency fund is crucial for weathering the storm of hyperinflation. By taking steps such as starting small with savings, automating the process, exploring ways to save, resisting the temptation to spend the funds, keeping them safe and accessible, continuously growing the fund, and diversifying with stable currency and a plan, individuals can increase their chances of surviving hyperinflation with a readily available source of cash to cover unexpected expenses and avoid incurring additional debt.

7. Prioritizing necessities over luxuries

By prioritizing necessities over luxuries, you can save money.

It is a fundamental human instinct to prioritize survival over luxury, but at times, having bad habits or addictions, eating out, or poor financial decisions can lead to mismanagement of funds during hyperinflation. In Iraq, the focus shifted to only putting food on the table, as luxury became a distant memory. The key to effectively managing funds during hyperinflation is to prioritize necessities over luxuries in the years leading to it. This proactive approach ensures that funds are allocated wisely, in the form of stable currency or long-term necessities, and enables individuals to withstand the pressure and skyrocketing prices brought on by hyperinflation. I recall a time when even white bread became a luxury in Iraq. But, people used humor and jokes to deal with such hardships they faced. By prioritizing necessities for at least two years before hyperinflation, individuals can effectively prepare for inevitable financial crises.

Here are some examples& tips for how to effectively prioritize necessities over luxuries that currently can still be applied in the western world before the actual times of hyperinflation:

1. **Make a budget**: Make a budget and track expenses to identify areas where money is being wasted. Cut back on unnecessary expenses and use the extra money to pay for necessities.

2. **Prioritize essential expenses**: Prioritize essential expenses, such as food, housing, healthcare, and transportation, over non-essential expenses, such as dining out, entertainment, and buying unnecessary stuff.

3. **Shop for deals**: Shop for deals and discounts on necessities, coupons and shop at discount stores.

4. **Buy in bulk**: Buy in bulk when possible to save money on necessities like food and household items.

5. **Cook at home**: Cook at home instead of eating out to save money on food expenses.

6. **Reduce energy consumption**: Reduce energy consumption by turning off lights and appliances when they are not in use, and looking for ways to save on utility bills.

7. **Avoid unnecessary travel**: Avoid unnecessary travel and stick to budget-friendly options when traveling is necessary, such as using public transportation, cheaper gas, etc.

8. **Look for alternatives**: Look for alternatives to necessities that are more affordable, such as using public transportation instead of driving or buying used clothing instead of new.

To summarize, focusing on necessities rather than luxuries is a crucial tactic for navigating hyperinflation. By creating a budget, prioritizing essential expenses, seeking deals, bulk buying, cooking at home, cutting energy use, avoiding non-essential travel, and finding alternatives, individuals can increase their chances of surviving hyperinflation by effectively utilizing their funds to cover their most important needs.

8. Building relationships with merchants:

Building relationships with merchants can provide access to goods and services at more favorable prices.

Building relationships with merchants is a crucial strategy to navigate hyperinflation as it can lead to more favorable prices for goods and services. However, the success of this strategy depends on various factors, such as the merchants' flexibility to help and the duration of their assistance. Merchants themselves are also affected by hyperinflation, especially under the pressure of recession and debt repayment to lenders. In rural areas and small towns, the capacity to implement this strategy may vary as the local community is smaller and may have greater flexibility for direct deals or access to goods straight from production. This has been observed in Iraq, where rural communities have had better chances to survive hyperinflation than urban centers.

Here are some ideas for how to effectively build relationships with merchants during times of hyperinflation:

1. **Shop locally**: Shop locally and get to know the merchants in your community. Building relationships with local merchants can provide access to goods and services at more favorable prices.

2. **Be loyal**: Be a loyal customer, and merchants may be more willing to offer discounts or special deals.

3. **Pay in cash**: Paying in cash can sometimes result in a lower price than paying with a credit or debit card.

4. **Be respectful**: Be respectful of the merchant's time and be willing to negotiate prices in a friendly and professional manner.

5. **Be flexible**: Be flexible with your shopping schedule and be willing to shop during off-peak hours for better deals.

6. **Take advantage of loyalty programs**: Take advantage of loyalty programs offered by merchants, such as rewards or cash back programs.

7. **Provide feedback**: Provide feedback on products or services to help merchants improve and build a better relationship.

8. **Shop at wholesale markets**: Shop at wholesale markets to get goods and services at bulk prices.

In short, cultivating relationships with merchants is a key approach to coping with hyperinflation as it can secure access to goods and services at more advantageous prices. To increase the chances of survival during hyperinflation, one can shop locally, establish loyalty as a customer, pay in cash, show respect, be flexible, utilize loyalty programs, provide constructive feedback, and buy in bulk at wholesale markets. Additionally, smaller towns and rural areas may offer a better environment for implementing this strategy, as they often have fewer people and greater supply chain flexibility. It's important to keep in mind that building relationships takes time and effort, but the long-term benefits are well worth it during economic difficulties.

9. Keeping informed about government policies

Keeping informed about government policies and regulations can provide information about what assistance may be available.

The Arabic proverb "Knowledge is light and ignorance is darkness" perfectly encapsulates the purpose of this point. Nothing has more potential to liberate society than knowledge and transparency. Thus, staying informed about government policies is crucial in navigating hyperinflation, as it provides insights into potential economic developments, especially when the economy is heavily influenced by political and central banking decisions, such as Iraq in the 90s. Government policies have a significant impact on the economy and can affect access to goods and services, prices, and the cost of living. Although the Iraqi government's centralized ration program for preventing starvation during a crisis and the UN's "Oil for Food" program had positive effects despite corruption, gaining critical information about government policies can be challenging due to the level of transparency and type of government. However, knowledge remains a powerful tool for individuals to arm themselves with.

Here are some examples, tips, and ideas for how to effectively keep yourself informed about government policies during times of hyperinflation:

1. **Follow official government websites and social media accounts**: Follow official government websites and social media accounts to stay updated on the latest policies and regulations.

2. **Stay informed about inflation data**: Stay informed about inflation data and monitor how it is affecting the cost of living.

3. **Monitor the exchange rate**: Monitor the exchange rate and how it affects the value of the local currency.

4. **Watch for policy changes**: Watch for policy changes that may affect prices, such as changes in taxes or subsidies.

5. **Learn about financial assistance programs:** Learn about financial assistance programs that may be available to help with the cost of living or debt repayment.

6. **Attend government meetings or hearings**: Attend government meetings or hearings to stay informed about policy changes and ask questions.

7. **Read official publications and reports**: Read official publications and reports to stay informed about policy changes and their implications.

8. **Connect with advocacy groups or non-profit organizations**: Connect with advocacy groups or non-profit organizations that can provide information about government policies and how they affect specific groups or individuals.

Staying informed about government policies is crucial for navigating hyperinflation. It provides insight into potential economic developments and access to assistance programs. One can stay informed by following official government websites and social media, monitoring inflation data, exchange rates, and policy changes, being aware of financial assistance programs, attending government meetings/hearings, reading official publications and reports, and connecting with advocacy groups. This increases the chances of surviving hyperinflation by understanding the measures taken to address it and explore available assistance.

10.

Preparing for emergencies

Preparing for emergencies by stockpiling non-perishable food, water, and other supplies can help reduce dependency on cash.

Preparing for emergencies is crucial to surviving hyperinflation because it can reduce the reliance on cash. During hyperinflation, the prices of goods and services can skyrocket, making it challenging to purchase essential items such as food and water. The subject of preparing for hyperinflation is extensive and cannot be fully covered in one page or a few steps. A comprehensive guide would be required to explain the various preparations that individuals can make and the details involved. The preparations must be specific and have clear goals, with a focus on the most essential items, only that are likely to be in short supply in the short term. These items should be acquired gradually and within one's budget. It is important to maintain a sufficient supply level at all times. This will be useful when trade stops and the supplies are used, and one will be amazed at how quickly they can be depleted despite constant shopping.

The importance of being prepared for hyperinflation:

1. It can save you a significant amount of money by allowing you to purchase essential items before prices skyrocket.
2. The items can be used as a form of currency to trade with friends and family for other goods.
3. Being prepared can help maintain your health and mental well-being during the difficult times of hyperinflation.
4. The essential items can be sold to others in need, potentially yielding a profit.
5. Preparation can provide a sense of security in the event of social unrest, revolution, war, or civil war, as seen in Iraq.
6. It can help people in remote areas who cannot afford or access necessary goods due to high fuel prices or unsafe conditions.
7. Being prepared can serve as a tool to assist others and save lives in times of need.
8. Finally, preparing for hyperinflation can help individuals understand the true value of life when money becomes meaningless, and the basic necessities such as food and companionship becomes important.

In Iraq, hyperinflation and wars, followed by revolution and martial law, have taught people the value of preparation. Money loses its value when it cannot be spent, when market closed, or it is worth nothing. Understanding the fundamentals of life and being prepared can be a lifesaver for many who have been too focused on material wealth and collecting money instead.

My dad was an intelligent and well-educated person who prepared ahead of time. I recall going with him to a wholesale market where we bought bulk quantities of essential items for daily use and survival, such as flour, rice, and oil. He also included high-calorie items like traditional Iraqi dates and nuts. When I asked him why he decided to get these items, he explained that they are a long-term savings that can sustain you without the need for cooking, which proved to be true six months later during a period of war, chaos and scarcity of cooking gas.

Here are some universal tips, and ideas for how to effectively prepare for emergencies during times of hyperinflation:

1. **Stockpile non-perishable food**: Stockpile non-perishable food, such as canned goods, dried fruits, and nuts, to ensure that you have enough to eat in case of an emergency.

2. **Build an emergency kit**: Build an emergency kit with items such as a flashlight, batteries, first aid supplies, and cash.

3. **Consider your water supply and plan accordingly,**: Whether it be through purchasing water filters or finding a method to store water. This subject requires further investigation as the options vary based on personal circumstances.

4. **Learn to live off the grid**: Learn to live off the grid, such as how to cook without electricity, in case of power outages.

5. **Have a garden**: Having a garden to grow your own food is always the best solution.

6. **Learn basic skills**: Learn basic skills, such as sewing, to be able to repair clothes and other items.

7. **Store medication**: Store medication and other essentials, such as hygiene products, in case of supply disruptions.

In conclusion, preparation for emergencies is a crucial aspect in surviving hyperinflation and other emergencies, whether they are natural, financial, or man-made such as wars or invasions. The stability of a city or country can quickly change due to unexpected events, like the global pandemic of 2020, making it important to be ready. By stockpiling non-perishable food, water, and other supplies, creating an emergency kit, planning for off-grid living, starting a garden, learning basic skills, and storing essential medications, individuals can increase their chances of survival. I encourage everyone to research and prioritize preparation for at least one month to bring peace of mind to themselves and their loved ones. Being prepared can bring a sense of security and reduce stress during challenging times.

Conclusion

Hyperinflation is a difficult economic phenomenon that can have a devastating impact on people's lives. It is characterized by rapid and uncontrolled increases in the prices of goods and services, which can make it difficult for people to afford basic necessities like food and housing. In order to survive hyperinflation, people need to make significant changes to their lifestyles and habits.

One of the most important things to consider during hyperinflation is the management of finances. This includes budgeting, cost management, building savings, increasing income, diversifying income, reducing debt, and building an emergency fund. These steps are crucial in reducing dependency on cash and preserving wealth during times of hyperinflation. Additionally, people should prioritize necessities over luxuries, building relationships with merchants, and staying informed about government policies and regulations, in order to access goods and services at more favorable prices.

It's important to note that, hyperinflation times can be very difficult, and it takes serious change in life habits, style of living in order to survive it, but it's not impossible and it's worth it. Once the economy stabilizes, the hard work and sacrifices made during the hyperinflation period will pay off.

Furthermore, my own experience in Iraq during hyperinflation has taught me that having precious metals, such as gold, can be a valuable asset during hyperinflation. It can act as a store of value and can be used to support the living standard in general. It's a good idea to have some gold pieces as a form of savings, so it can be used in case of emergency.

In conclusion, hyperinflation is a difficult economic phenomenon that requires significant changes to one's lifestyle and habits in order to survive. However, by taking the necessary steps such as financial management, prioritizing necessities, and preparing for emergencies, people can increase their chances of surviving hyperinflation and waiting for the prosperous times afterwards.